Published By

Hugo Publishing Company
128 East Jackson Street
Hugo, Okla. 74743

© 2019

ISBN # 978-0-9882646-6-3

Dedication...

For Jonathan
and
the Lacy Family

Sitting on the
stoop with
Meredith...

...She told me
about her
dream...

I dreamt
of a
Spider.

It made
me
scared.

It had
a
mustache.

It was
long
like a
beard.

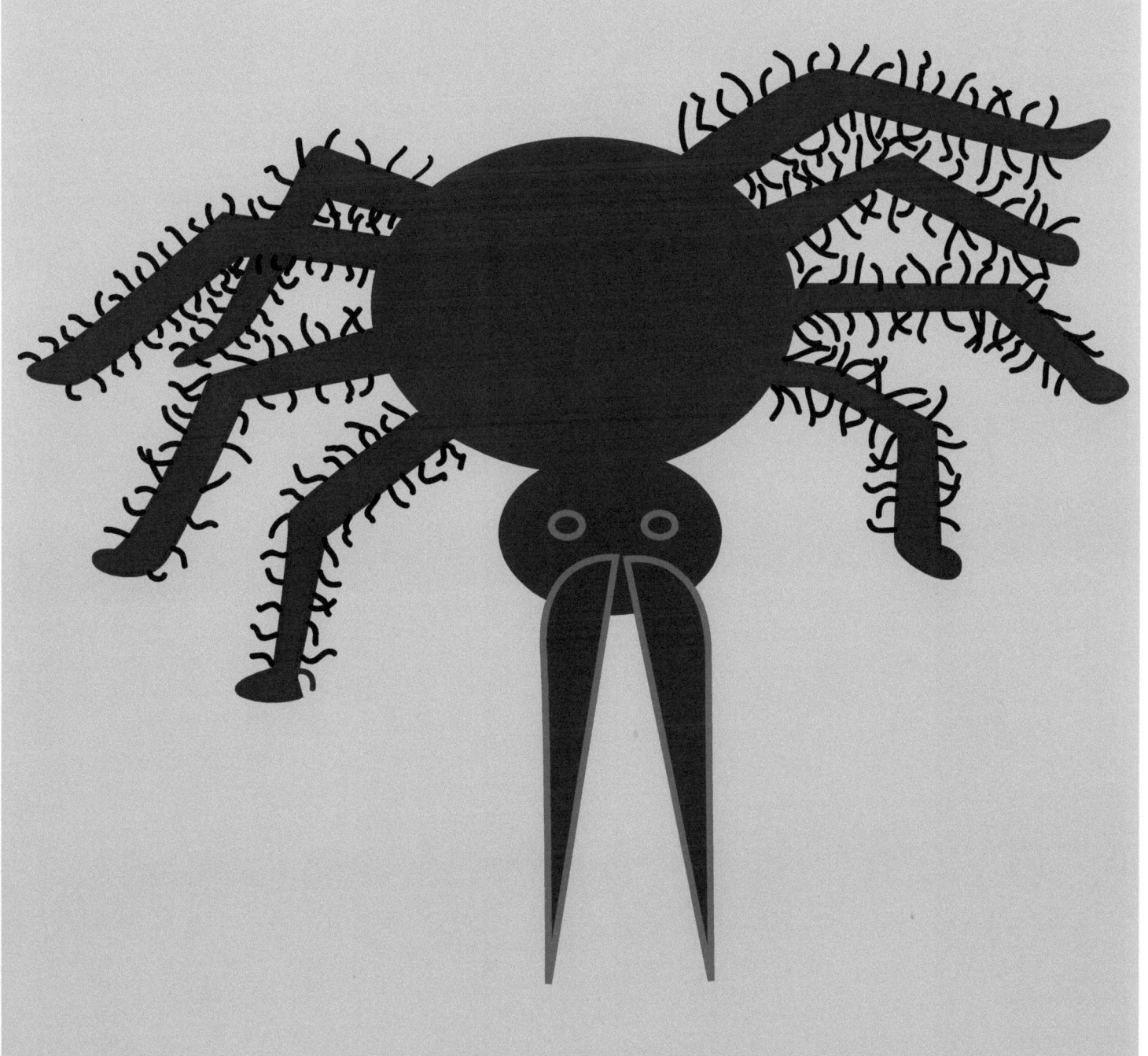

All 8 legs were long and hairy.

In my dream... ...it was really scary!

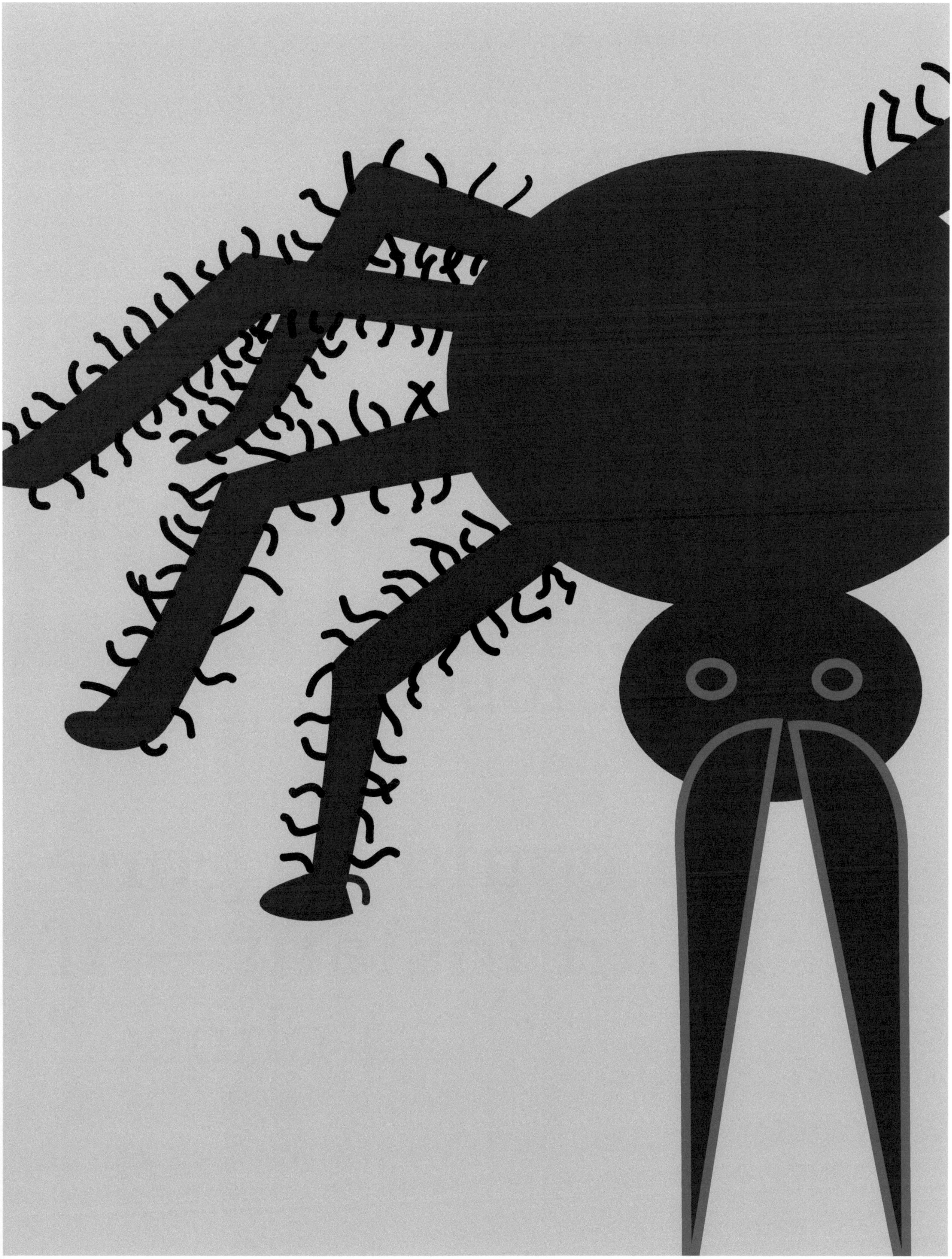

I remember
Dad saying...

"With one eye open
and one eye
closed...

...it could be gone
in an instant — if
I chose."

Giving him a chance...

I closed both my eyes...

...and asked him to DANCE!

What a sight
it was to see...

...twirling
like he was
in a
Jamboree!

Two legs
here...

Two legs
there.

Four legs
dancing
in a square.

In the midst
of all the fun,
up in the sky
was the morning
sun.

Beckoning me
to open
my eyes...

was Mom's voice...
"It is time to rise!"

The
End!

I dreamt of a spider
It made me scared.

It had a mustache
It was long like a beard.

All eight legs were long and hairy
In my dream it was really scary

With one eye open and one eye closed
He could be gone in an instant if I chose.

Giving him a chance
I closed both eyes and asked him to dance.

What a sight it was to see,
Twirling like he was in a Jamboree.

Two legs here.
Two legs there.
Four legs dancing in a square.

In the midst of all the fun
Up in the sky was the morning sun.

Beckoning me to open my eyes
Was Mom's voice: "It is time to rise."

VOCABULARY

Stoop —	A step in a stair.
Mustache —	The hairs growing on the upper lip.
Beard —	The growth of hair on the face of an adult man.
Twirling —	Rotate rapidly; spin.
Midst —	The middle part.
Jamboree —	Noisy merry merrymaking; party, a bash, a festival.
Beckoning —	to lure; entice.

CPSIA information can be obtained
at www.ICGtesting.com
Printed in the USA
BVHW021334071119
563179BV00009B/181/P